Your Amazing Itty Bitty® Guide to a Balanced Life

15 Key Steps to Building a Balanced Life

Life is a balancing act. You balance so many things on a day-to-day basis: Family, Relationships, Career, and Health; just to name a few. This Itty Bitty® book is a guide to help you achieve that balance. It covers all areas of your life with an emphasis on health.

Follow along with Dr. Jody Jones as she takes you through the steps to align and harmonize your life. As one area falls into place the others will naturally follow.

In this book you will be able to set the scales to find balance in the areas of:

- Health Care
- Nutrition
- Mindset
- and so much more!

If you're looking for balance and harmony, pick up a copy of this life changing book today.

Your Amazing Itty Bitty®
Guide to a Balanced Life

15 Key Steps to Building a Balanced Life

Dr. Jody Jones

Published by Itty Bitty® Publishing
A subsidiary of S & P Productions, Inc.

Copyright © 2021 **Jody Jones, DNP, CNP**

All rights reserved. No part of this book may be reproduced or transmitted in any form or by any means, electronic or mechanical, including photocopying, recording, or by any information storage and retrieval system, without written permission of the publisher, except for inclusion of brief quotations in a review.

Printed in the United States of America

Itty Bitty Publishing
311 Main Street, Suite D
El Segundo, CA 90245
(310) 640-8885

ISBN: 978-1-950326-14-3

This information is for educational purposes only and is not intended as a substitute for medical advice, diagnosis, or treatment. You should not use this information to diagnose, or to treat a health problem or condition. Always check with your doctor before changing your diet, altering your sleep habits, taking supplements, or starting a new fitness routine.

Dedication

This book never would have been made possible without the love and support of my dear husband and soulmate, Jody Dodge. Thank you, my love, for always believing in me and teaching me the true meaning of BALANCE. Will love you always and forever. May our lives be balanced and in sync together forever.

Stop by our Itty Bitty® website to find interesting blog entries regarding being balanced and more!

www.IttyBittyPublishing.com

Or visit Balance with Dr. Jody at

www.balancewithdrjody.com

Table of Contents

Introduction
Step 1.   What is Balance?
Step 2.   Balance Your Mind With Meditation
Step 3.   Balance Your Gut
Step 4.   Balance Your Weight
Step 5.   Balance Your Sleep
Step 6.   Balance Your Hydration
Step 7.   Balance Your Nutrition
Step 8.   Balance Your Stress
Step 9.   Balance Your Immune System
Step 10. Balance Your Dreams
Step 11. Balance Your Relationships
Step 12. Balance Your Health Care
Step 13. Balance Your Finances
Step 14. Balance Your Fitness
Step 15. Balance Your Self

Introduction

Life is a balancing act. We all balance so many things in our day-to-day lives! Family, relationships, career, health, just to name a few. This book is about how to gain control and achieve balance in a variety of different areas of your life, with an emphasis on health.

Following these simple steps will set you on the right course for achieving and feeling balance.

> For more information, please check out
> www.balancewithdrjody.com.

Step 1
What is BALANCE?
BALANCE Defined

BALANCE: Be You! Always Love and Never Compromise. Ever!

Balance is both a noun and a verb. As a noun, balance is defined as, "a state of equilibrium or equipoise; something used to produce equilibrium." As a verb, it is defined as, "to arrange, adjust, or proportion the parts of, symmetrically." (www.dictionary.com)

1. The first step in any process is being ready to change. Once you are ready to change just one area of your life, the rest will fall into place.
2. This book is a guide to the primary areas of your health which, when balanced, will lead to clarity and symmetry in your life.
3. Follow along each step and watch how life unfolds! As one area falls into alignment, others naturally follow suit.

Remember, do not rush the process. Sometimes one area takes more effort than others. Honor each step and remember to enjoy the journey! It will all be worth it in the end!

TIPS: Why BALANCE?

- BALANCE is all about equilibrium and symmetry in your life.
- This program is designed with an emphasis on health.
- Balancing multiple areas of your life will lead to improvement in physical, mental, emotional, and financial health, to name a few.

Step 2
Balance Your Mind

The mind is a powerful tool. On average, you only use 5% of your brain. That leaves 95% of your brain completely untouched! How wonderful would it be to increase the utilization from 5% to even 10%? Think about what your life would look like then!

1. Changing your mind involves regular meditation.
2. Meditation is about slowing the mind and becoming present.
3. It is an ongoing process, yet you will absolutely reap the benefits by practicing consistently.
4. Meditation will increase the utilization of your brain cells rather quickly.

TIPS: How to Balance Your Mind

- Start slowly! Starting with a two - to five - minute meditation is perfect. Progress as your brain is able to do so.
- Set aside the same time every day for your meditation.
- Allow for uninterrupted time and space.
- Notify your family about this commitment to prevent further interruptions.
- Ensure you do not have children, spouses/partners, or animals interrupting you.
- Turn your phone off - or better yet, leave it in another room.
- If you use your phone for meditation, turn it on airplane mode to prevent interruptions.

Step 3
Balance Your Gut

The intestinal tract (GI tract) starts at the mouth and ends at the rectum. Disease, or "dis-ease," can occur anywhere throughout the GI tract.

1. Commonly referred to as the stomach, the GI tract actually has multiple parts and systems.
2. Each area has a specific role in digestion, absorption, and excretion of food.
3. If one area is out of balance, the entire system can become disrupted.
4. The GI tract is filled with good bacteria, commonly referred to as the microbiome.
5. Food, medications, illness, or stress can disrupt the system and cause unpleasant symptoms.

TIPS to Balance Your Gut

- It starts with food! Every single thing that passes through your mouth affects your overall health.
- Food is a choice. All food is either healthy or not healthy. Food is not neutral.
- Take a daily probiotic to reset the good bacteria in the intestinal tract.
- Probiotics maintain healthy bowels.
- Having a bowel movement after each meal is healthy.

Step 4
Balance Your Weight

An imbalance in your weight may be a symptom of an underlying problem. Being overweight can lead to a multitude of chronic diseases. Being underweight is also just as detrimental to your health as well.

1. Talk to your health care provider about a healthy weight range.
2. Create a plan together with your health care provider to achieve your healthy weight in a realistic period of time.
3. Be realistic with the time needed to achieve your determined goal. Weight fluctuations did not occur overnight and will not resolve overnight!
4. Weight maintenance is lifelong and may prevent chronic disease.

TIPS to Balance Your Weight

- Identify your healthy weight range.
- Your ideal weight may not be the same as a healthy weight; this is okay!
- Be realistic in your time frame. A healthy weight loss is 0.5-2 pounds per week.
- Fad diets are only temporary; seek a program which teaches long-lasting habit changes and healthy lifestyle choices.
- Create a support system for your journey. Research supports that a buddy or group increases compliance and long-term success for weight maintenance.

Step 5
Balance Your Sleep

Not enough credit is given to the importance of sleep. The average adult needs 7-9 hours of sleep each night in order to regenerate and recharge; children need more sleep. Due to multiple commitments and our busy lives, you may be foregoing sleep for work or family commitments. This is ultimately detrimental to your health.

1. The ideal time for you to be in bed is by 10:30 PM. Going to bed later than this disrupts the natural circadian rhythm.
2. Melatonin is naturally produced as the sun goes down and this causes drowsiness to occur. Listen to your body! When you feel sleepy, start to unwind and get ready for bed.
3. Serotonin is a hormone which is produced as the sun rises. This allows us to wake naturally. Similar to melatonin, listen to your body. Get out of bed when your body starts to wake up!

TIPS to Balance Your Sleep

- Go to sleep at the same time every night.
- The ideal time to be in bed is no later than 10:30PM.
- Wake at the same time every morning; try to wake naturally!
- It is ideal for you to wake with the sun rather than an alarm clock.
- Taking melatonin at bedtime will help you with sleep.
- Avoid prescription sleep aids as these do not lead to the restorative sleep necessary.
- Remove electronics from the bedroom.

Step 6
Balance Your Intake of Beverages

Water is essential to your livelihood. All cells and organs of the body rely on water for your survival. When out of balance, water intake is less than your output, and dehydration occurs.

1. Drinking fluids helps maintain the balance of your body fluids.
2. Drinking water can help decrease caloric intake.
3. Drinking water keeps your skin looking healthy.
4. Drinking water helps with excretion of urine and also maintaining healthy bowels.

TIPS to Balance Your Intake of Beverages

- Drink pure, clean filtered water.
- Do not allow plastic water bottles to be in heat; drinking from glass bottles is preferred.
- Avoid or minimize caffeine and alcohol, as these can be dehydrating.
- Determine your weight in pounds; divide in two. This is the number of ounces of water to drink daily.
- Increase your water intake with heavy exercise to replace fluids lost.
- Drinking products made with water do not count as water. Your body will recognize this as food and you are not receiving the same benefit you get from good, clean, filtered water.

Step 7
Balance Your Nutrition

Balancing your nutrition is definitely a juggling act. Figuring out the perfect plan for each individual can be a bit of a challenge. However, once this has been accomplished, it leads to lifelong health. It is definitely worth your time and energy to figure out how to balance your nutrition!

1. Eat real food! If a food item was not in the grocery store during your grandparents' generation, do not eat it.
2. Eat from the rainbow. The more colorful fruits and vegetables you eat, the healthier!
3. Stay attuned to your feelings which occur after eating. Healthy foods will give a person energy and clarity; unhealthy foods will lead to fatigue, feeling bloated, and other physical symptoms.
4. What works for one person may not work for another. Nutrition is very individualized.

TIPS to Balance Your Nutrition

- Eat organic foods when possible.
- Eat foods without nutrition labels; this is the way food was designed.
- Shop locally—preferably from a farmer's market if available. If not, consider a delivery service for fresh produce and meat.
- Be sure to drink enough fluids during the day with an emphasis on clean, pure water.
- Avoid processed sugar and artificial sweeteners.
- Consider working with a health care provider who specializes in nutrition to create a plan just for you.

Step 8
Balance Your Stress

Stress can come in the form of a negative stressor such as losing a job, ending a relationship or dealing with a disease. Stress can also come in the form of a positive, such as winning the lottery. Your brain is unable to differentiate negative stress from positive stress.

1. Meditation calms the mind and will reduce stress.
2. Factors which cause stress include illness, not sleeping well, or an imbalance in your work/life, to name a few.
3. Too much exercise can be stressful on your body as well. More often than not, more is not better.

TIPS to Balance Your Stress

- Meditate daily to decrease your stress.
- Exercise daily to reduce your stress. Recommendation is 20 minutes per day of movement.
- Balance your workouts to prevent fatigue and stress on your body.
- Maintain a balance with work and life. Working too much and not allowing time with your family, or self-love, are very detrimental to your health.

Step 9
Balance Your Immune System

The majority of your immune system is actually found in the gastrointestinal (GI) system, commonly called the gut. If your gut health is compromised, this can lead to a decrease in the immune system.

1. Many people associate winter with "flu season." Influenza and other infections are more prevalent in the winter seasons due to being inside more, having more contact with people who may be infectious, as well as the mindset of "flu season."
2. Balancing your immune system includes changing the mindset from, "I always get the flu every December," to a positive affirmation, such as, "I am healthy all year long!"
3. Ensuring adequate nutrition and fluid intake also boosts your immune system.

TIPS to Balance Your Immune System

- Minimize your stress.
- Ensure adequate sleep; recommendation is 7-9 hours per night for an adult. Children need more sleep.
- Utilize high-quality supplements all year round such as vitamin C, vitamin D, zinc and probiotics to prevent infection.
- Increase your supplements at the earliest sign of an infection.
- Minimize use of antibiotics unless absolutely necessary.
- Follow-up with your health care professional with any questions or concerns regarding an infection.

Step 10
Balance Your Dreams

Dreaming is essential for creating the life you desire. Thoughts become reality and words are very powerful.

1. Visualization of your dreams is a very powerful tool. Being vague with dreams will lead to uncertainty coming forward from the universe.
2. Utilization of words is just as important as the visualization. Make statements such as, "I am," instead of, "I want." Stating, "I want," just leads to more wanting.
3. Take the time to do soul searching for what brings you joy and happiness—and follow through on it!!

TIPS to Balance Your dreams

- Create a vision board which encompasses both your personal and professional dreams.
- Place the vision board in an area with a lot of visibility. Seeing it daily will help you begin to manifest your dreams.
- Be specific! Visualizing and asking for specific items will bring more success.
- Be playful! Have fun with your vision board!

Step 11
Balance Your Relationships

Humans are very social. Relationships are an essential part of being human.

1. Lack of human contact and relationships lead to a suppressed immune system, and ultimately, an increased risk of infection.
2. Evaluate your current relationships. Choose to keep healthy relationships. For unhealthy relationships, bless that person with love and light and then release them. The universe will bring forward healthier relationships in time.
3. Relationships of any sort, friendship, professional, or even family, can all be evaluated. Do what is best for you right now. Your body and the universe will thank you!

TIPS to Balance Your Relationships

- Take an inventory of the people in your life.
- Evaluate which relationships are healthy and which may be unhealthy.
- Seek professional help for counseling or other therapy as needed.

Step 12
Balance Your Health Care Needs

All individuals have health care needs at all ages. It is important to remember to have your annual physical examination during which screenings occur for diseases as well as education to prevent diseases.

1. Schedule your health care maintenance exam (annual physical). The recommendation is annually for adults; the recommendations for children vary based on age.
2. Your health care also includes dental exams every six months and an annual eye exam for individuals in need of contacts lenses or glasses.
3. Chronic health conditions require additional visits. Consult your health care provider for recommendations on frequency of visits.

TIPS to Balance Your Health Care Needs

- Maintain or create a relationship with a health care provider, dentist, and eye doctor if indicated.
- Follow-up annually for your routine health maintenance needs.
- Follow-up as directed for management of chronic health diseases if indicated.
- Consider alternative sources of care in addition to your routine health care such as chiropractic care, acupuncture, and/or massage therapy. Be creative! Create a team that works for you!

Step 13
Balance Your Financial Health

Financial health is a component of living a healthy, balanced life. Being financially unbalanced can lead to stress which can lead to "dis-ease."

1. When deciding to lose weight, the first step is to determine the starting weight. When deciding to balance your finances, the first step is to determine how much is coming in on a monthly basis and how much is going out. Your first step is to write down how much is coming in and how much is going out in one month.
2. Financial health can cause some unwanted emotions to surface. This is a normal part of the process; allow the feelings and speak to your health care provider if needed.
3. Financial planners are wonderful resources not only helping to plan for retirement yet also assisting with day-to-day budgeting, spending and savings suggestions.

TIPS for Balancing Your Financial Health

- Count your money! It is hard to determine your financial status without knowing your starting point.
- Create a spending plan. Remember, a spending plan is one month at a time and can be adjusted at any time.
- Put your money away in a savings account on a regular basis.
- Anybody can save more money! It is just simply changing your habits. Start with putting away money on a weekly basis and watching it accrue. It works and it's easy!
- Maximize your employer's retirement plan; the money saved is pre-tax and definitely an easy way to save money.

Step 14
Balance your Fitness/Exercise

Maintaining physical fitness is one more piece of the puzzle. Physical fitness boosts the immune system, improves sleep, and can assist with either weight loss or weight maintenance.

1. Physical fitness is very individualized. No two people respond the same way to the same exercise. Therefore, it is important to create a personalized program.
2. Personal trainers are a wonderful resource for setting up a program as well as working with on an ongoing basis if this is something of interest to you.
3. Consider taking a class. Many people respond well to a group fitness environment.

TIPS for Balancing Your Fitness/Exercise

- Identify an activity which you enjoy. Doing something that is not fun, or which you consider work, will not be sustainable.
- Taking measurements, including body fat, at the beginning of any fitness program is essential to tracking your progress. Be sure to measure on a monthly basis.
- Consider working with a personal trainer to create a personalized plan.
- Set a goal! Consider completing a local race, participating in a new activity, or entering a competition of some sort.

Step 15
Balance Your Spirit

Balancing your spirit is the final step of this Itty Bitty® Book. BALANCE is all about self-love and embracing ALL areas of self, including mind, body, and spirit.

1. Loving self is the core of BALANCE with Dr. Jody and this book. Integral to self-love is the piece of embracing spirit.
2. Being able to identify and connect with your spirit is essential for balance. This will come in time by following the above steps with an emphasis on meditation.
3. Taking care of yourself is essential before you are able to take care of others.

TIPS for Balancing Your Spirit

- Once a week, set a goal of self-love. Some examples include sleeping in one morning, taking a bath, reading a book, or spending time with a loved one.
- Practice Steps 2-15 as outlined in this book, and your spirit will begin to fall into place and become balanced.
- Pay extra attention to meditation and manifesting your dreams.
- Create your vision board and watch your reality come true!
- Remember, thoughts DO become reality.

You've finished. Before you go ...

Tweet/share that you finished this book.

Please star rate this book.

Reviews are solid gold to writers. Please take a few minutes to give us some itty bitty feedback.

ABOUT THE AUTHOR

All her life, Dr. Jody Jones knew she wanted to be a nurse. Was it her destiny, as she was dressed up as a nurse at the ripe old age of 18 months for a Christmas card, or was it in her blood? It doesn't matter; all she knows is her calling has been to take care of people.

Dr. Jody lives in southern California with her husband, Jody and their three four-legged fur babies. She has been a nurse since 1989, a Nurse Practitioner since 1999, and completed her Doctorate in Nursing Practice in 2011.

As a transplant from Minnesota, she enjoys all that California has to offer, including spending much time at the ocean, which is how she finds balance in her life. She and Jody enjoy traveling all over the state, creating incredible meals together, and sharing the "Jody Squared" story and products.

If you liked this Itty Bitty® Book
you might also enjoy:

- **Your Amazing Itty Bitty® Heal Your Body Book** – Patricia Garza Pinto

- **Your Amazing Itty Bitty® Diet Free Weight Loss Book** – Elizabeth "Liz" Bull

- **Your Amazing Itty Bitty® Stress Reduction Book** – Denise Thomson

Or many of the other many Itty Bitty® books
available on line at
www.ittybittypublishing.com.

www.ingramcontent.com/pod-product-compliance
Lightning Source LLC
Chambersburg PA
CBHW061305040426
42444CB00010B/2524